THIRTY THREE DAYS

A POETRY JOURNAL

GUILLERMO NODARSE

FIRST PUBLISHED IN 2001 BY

Numen Press Inc.
P.O. Box 357
Winter Park, Florida 32790-0357

Printed in the United States of America

ISBN: 0-9707688-0-X

For

LEILA JAMMAL NODARSE,

ALEJANDRO OCTAVIO NODARSE,

and

FRANCISCO LEONIDES NODARSE,

with all my love;

and to

my mother, **OLGA SERRA NODARSE**, who has
taught me the meaning of humor,
strength, and unconditional love.

Acknowledgements

There are many people I feel indebted to,
for their constant kindness and support; what follows
is a very abbreviated list of some of those individuals.
Thanks to Dr. Keith and Joan McKean for their steadfast
encouragement; to Dr. Adolfo Franco who has taken the
time to review all my works and to offer constructive feed-
back; to Dr. George Day for his support; to Terry
Brennan, who has shown me once again that
true friends are not always a product of the length of
time of a friendship; to Cheryl Haley, for her superb
administrative skills; to each of my family members,
who bless me daily with their love; and finally to my
father and mentor, Dr. Samuel Nodarse, whose unfailing
enthusiasm for life enlightens all who know him.

Preface

Dear Reader,

Poetry is the Song of the Soul. For thirty-three days I have
tried to be open to my song, and this book represents that
effort. I hope you enjoy these poems, and that they, in some
small way, encourage you to be receptive to your unique music
as well.

G.N.

Table of Contents

Table of Contents

Table of Contents

Table of Contents

Table of Contents

You must concentrate upon and
consecrate yourself wholly to each
day, as though a fire were raging
in your hair.

DESHIMARU

This is the day which the Lord has
      made;
    let us rejoice and be glad in it.

PSALMS 118:24

Tuesday, September 12, 2000

EARLY MORNING

$\mathcal{I}$ went to the lake early this morning. There were four Old People sitting on the dock, smoking, talking to the alligator that lives by the shore. They said, "Don't grow old - why don't you jump in?" The alligator smiled. It was inviting, but I had to finish my toast first.

PARTICULAR HABITS

$\mathcal{I}$ sat down in front of our house. We have little white chairs there, arranged to look at one another; otherwise they get bored. The gray owl sat in his usual place, and shook his head. "You're doing it all wrong. First eat the worms, *then* drink the lake water." Like all of us, he is particular about his habits.

Wednesday, September 13, 2000

MOVERS

The funeral home moved me out of the house, while I was still alive. They took my books, tore my letters, stepped on photographs. When they looked in my closet, they smiled - "He actually wore these shirts?" My wife nodded. She pointed at my boots. "And those too," she said, and they all shared a good belly laugh.

I sat nearby and drank cold water. What was wrong with my boots? I thought.

UNINVITED GUESTS

Sometimes words come up, unexpected, barbed and sharp. I don't know where they live, maybe in a railroad car that smells of urine, maybe a flop house where rooms rent for $10 a night. They come and go as they please, but leave a mess behind.

BEARDED LADY

$\mathcal{I}$ worked at a carnival once, taking tickets for the bearded lady. She dreamt in German. She had nightmares about losing her beard, but was proudest of her double chin.

Thursday, September 14, 2000

EMPTY FARMHOUSE

I remember walking up the gravel road. The moon followed, curious. The white farmhouse waved and invited us in for tea. We were joined by seven jars of pickled pigs feet, and they like their tea hot. So we sat and sipped tea in chipped cups, late at night in an empty Wisconsin farmhouse.

ENIGMA

We drove in circles around Pisa. The leaning tower leaned further, and swayed in the wind. It pointed to a way out, but we could never tell where its finger was. So we asked a row of prostitutes lined up like trees, and they laughed.

For Lee and Churchill

SADNESS

*S*adness came by the other day, dressed in a linen suit. He had just gotten a new haircut, and smelled of hotel cologne. "Mind if I join you?" he asked, and hoping not to be rude, I welcomed him in.

I hope he doesn't stay too long.

Friday, September 15, 2000

Friday, September 15, 2000

MY DOUBLE

My double popped in yesterday, just to make trouble. He does that now and then. The problem is, he always takes off his shoes, and his feet smell. He brought a bag of popcorn, and asked if I wanted any.

He said, "I'm bored. I'm here to watch your movie."

I said, "Go buy a ticket somewhere else."

UNCERTAINTY

*U*ncertainty lives in a small hole in my brain. He comes out early in the morning or late at night. I tell him he's getting predictable. He grins and says that's his nature.

SCARECROWS

The five scarecrows sat with me in the library, before the sun came up. When the crows are asleep. They read very little - once in awhile they pick up a magazine - but they love the armchairs. "These chairs are so comfortable," one of them rustles. I agree with him, and brush off the hay when they're gone.

Saturday, September 16, 2000

WORDS

$\mathcal{I}$ found a word the other day, beneath a red rock. It looked lonely, so I put it on my bookshelf next to other words. Late at night, they discuss matters of singular importance before nodding off.

Saturday, September 16, 2000

GODS

$\mathcal{T}$he Gods gathered around the conference table, in casual wear. "Do you remember when Bobby forgot to close the door, and the Universe ended?" asked the fat one at the end of the table.

They guffawed.

When Gods guffaw, we think it's thunder.

BIRTH

$\mathcal{D}$eath happens all the time. Birth shows up sparingly, particularly before the alarm clock rings, or when you bend down to tie your shoes. She likes to sneak up, and her perfume is strong.

INTERVIEW

*H*e had been dead for three years, and still chain smoked. He had big bags under his eyes. "It's not so bad. I'm always cold but I still get to go to the drive-in."

I asked him, Where could you still find a drive-in?

CLEAN-OUT

$\mathcal{T}$he chickens had been there a long time, before the Ice Age. They were comfortable, sitting above a river of chicken shit and smelling one another. We grabbed three at a time in each hand and carried them to the trucks outside. None wanted to go.

In the trucks they tried to understand what had happened.

For Bret Wrage

BLIND MAN

$\mathcal{I}$ sold vacuum cleaners one summer. I knocked on doors, got kicked out, and cleaned carpets. "Look how your vacuum isn't doing the job," I said. They nodded yes and pulled out their checkbooks.

I took the blind man's hands and rubbed them in the dirt pile. This is what your machine is missing, I told him. He understood and said no one treated him like a human being. So he bought two, and gave one to his cousin.

But he couldn't see his clean carpets.

Sunday, September 17, 2000

THREE WITCHES

The three witches wore fashionable skirts and high heels. They made their beds on cobblestone streets and smiled at me. I was only eleven, but could tell they were witches.

Their red lipstick gave them away.

REINCARNATION

Who says there is no reincarnation? I told the rain that, and the drops smiled.

"I landed on Caesar's cloak, when he crossed the Rubicon," said one.

"Cleopatra's sails were moistened by me and my brother, on the Nile," said another.

"I watered your garden, when you were a boy," said a third.

So I welcomed them home.

Sunday, September 17, 2000

LIGHTNING BUGS

At six o'clock sharp Mr. Moe opens his front door, and sets out two nylon chairs. His beer is very cold.

Down the street, George finishes raking the corner of their manicured lawn. Katie swears in German when her porcelain rooster shatters. Mike collects water bugs in a coffee can at the creek.

Everything makes sense just then. At six o'clock, on a summer night, in Cedar Falls. It is time, the lightning bugs agree, to show off their fall fashions.

We stand amazed.

For Don Moe

Monday, September 18, 2000

GONDOLIERS

*I*n a dream the Angel told me heaven was like Venice. We each have our own gondola, carved from dark wood. Some are painted, some are not. Dressed in blue silk, the gondoliers show us their backs. Canal water runs clear and sings Opera, beneath bridges of marble that shine like snow.

How about the Bridge of Sighs? I asked.

He looked puzzled. "There are no Sighs in Heaven," he answered.

ABUELA IN IOWA

My *abuela* had watery blue eyes and smelled of talcum. She made *melcocha* and placed it on strips of paper; its lemon taste stuck to my teeth.

As she grew older, sugar cane blossomed in Iowa, and farmers joked in Spanish.

One autumn morning, she opened the closet door, parted the winter coats, and left for home.

For Esther Fernandez Nodarse

LOVERS

The worm jumps into the mouth of its robin.
A grasshopper leaps into the mouth of its snake.
The fish springs into its net.

We are all made for one another.

RAT

Five in the morning. Clocks are dreaming. The Rat in the library wall licks the plaster and, Hungry, he only finds ghosts.

I overhear their whispered conversation.

Tuesday, September 19, 2000

EGO

*M*y ego tapped on the window so I let him in. His wings were wet. He was naked except for the new black socks.

"You've lost weight," I told him.

"I got these at a garage sale," he replied.

STREETOLOGY

*H*ere's how to read people. Forget horoscopes. Ask them what street they were born on.

Presidentials - Jefferson, Madison, Taylor, Washington - like to count, wear shirts with collars, and construct churches.

Trees - Elms, Acorns, Oaks - forget to wind their watches, get speeding tickets, and are firmly rooted.

Numbers - Third, Second, or Fifth - don't stay in Rotary long, since their minds are full of tomorrow.

So next time in a bar, ask them, "What's your Street?"

Wednesday, September 20, 2000

BOOK OF SOULS

*I*n the front closet of Heaven

God

keeps the Book of Souls. On rainy days

he

turns

its

Pages. He likes the feel

of

Parchment.

LOUD

How loud silence.

How loud a heartbeat.
How loud a thought.
How loud a gesture.
How loud a pause.

How loud.

Thursday, September 21, 2000

CEMETERY

*E*arly morning. As I lay
sleeping, the
tombstones gather together, and drink
their morning
coffee.

Friday, September 22, 2000

SEVEN DAYS

God created heaven and earth in seven days.
I can understand that.

On Monday, Francisco was born, chubby-cheeked and warm.
Four leaves fluttered onto our front lawn, red ants dragged
away a dead grasshopper, and rain came;

On Tuesday, the Oak tree shed a limb it was tired of, all
wrapped in moss, for our enjoyment. We didn't notice it.

On Wednesday, a caterpillar hunched its way to the top of a
fern in our front yard, tipping it until it bowed in gratitude;

On Thursday seven ducks circled our dock, playing tag;

On Friday, the lake turned red, a combination of early sun and
embarrassment from its previous night's behaviour;

On Saturday a new rose appeared in the garden;

On Sunday, the grass fell silent at the coming of the mower.

Seven days later, and it seems a year has passed.

For Francisco Leonides
on his first Birthday

Saturday, September 23, 2000

SUPPOSE

*S*uppose for a moment.
That only love was real.

Not the house you live in,
Or the job you work at,
Or the money you save,
Or the vacation you take,
Or the award you win.

Suppose for a moment.
That only love was real.

What would you do then?

Sunday, September 24, 2000

MOMENT, THIS

How small a moment, this:
At my desk
a lamp illuminates my thoughts
a tree limb plays with our bedroom window
my breath keeps time with the wind.

How rich a moment, this.

Monday, September 25, 2000

GOD'S IDEAS

God dreams in detail. Look at the
scars on a Cypress tree,
or the hair on a Squirrel's back,
or the Smell of garlic,
or the smile of a baby:

These are God's ideas.

Tuesday, September 26, 2000

BEACH

The Beach sleeps, waiting for
the coming of the
Water.
Starfish create Constellations,
Hermit Crabs argue over Housing,
and
Sand builds many-chambered Castles
begging for destruction.

I dream and listen to their song.

Wednesday, September 27, 2000

BUSINESS TRIP

*S*adness knocks hard on my bedroom door.
As usual, he's wearing white - that's his
favorite color. "It's time to pack your bags,"
he says.

So you make sure your toothpaste and
toothbrush are
there, and the razor blades, and the
deodorant.
You always want to smile and
smell nice.

"Could you stay behind?" I ask him, not wanting
his company.

He smiles and shakes his head. "I'd miss you too
much."

Thursday, September 28, 2000

INVITATION

$\mathcal{D}$eath sent me an invitation on white linen paper, with gilded Edges. (Death is very proper - he believes in proper etiquette.)

The note read,
>   Please Join Me Tomorrow for Tea, at
>   Two in the Afternoon.

I called him back. "What if I have a previous engagement?"

He said, "Don't worry, I make delicious tea."

Friday, September 29, 2000

RECOLLECTION

A small house with three iron deer near the front porch;
A kind-hearted woman who makes chocolate cakes, and
       serves them with cold milk from glass bottles;
A sleeping green lawn, without trace of a weed;
A silver clothesline, Singing in the sun;

A curious little boy.

A grace-filled church, with white cross;
A long vacant lot, rich in dandelions;
A Hornet's nest, waiting for the next flower;
A hard dirt-clod, formed for human hand;

A curious little boy.

An eye, closed for better accuracy;
An arm, flung skyward with earnestness;
A piece of earth, knocking down the sleeping tribe;
A darkness of maddened insects:

A curious little boy,
sprinting for salvation.

Saturday, September 30, 2000

DISCONNECT

I've got news for you:
I don't want your e-mail,
I don't want your fax,
I don't want to be beeped,
Voice-mailed, paged, prodded,
    Solicited, marketed to,
    Queried, categorized,
    Pigeon-holed, or
    analyzed.

You need to Disconnect to Reconnect.

I want to Reconnect.

Sunday, October 1, 2000

STARS

*A*t night when we sleep
God takes a giant bucket full of
Stars
and
Spills them onto a Black
Blanket.

GHOSTS

$\mathcal{I}$ was dining alone one evening when five Ghosts approached.
"Do you mind if we join you?" the eldest one asked.

Knowing how sensitive Ghosts are, I pulled out
five chairs and served them fresh mussels in white wine:
they dipped their French bread
in the broth.

Dinner was a huge success.

TRAIN WHISTLE

The Train whistled late at night, asking me to come and Play. Before I could reply, He had already left and taken His voice with Him.

Monday, October 2, 2000

LAKE

Our lake is an animal, disguised as water. At sunrise
It sheds its black
pelt and
reveals its true self.

Be careful.
It eats hours and days.

RIVER

Where does the River flow? I hear it
beneath the stone
floor, beyond the trimmed
lawn,
past the cut
flowers.

I hear it in the bats' wings,
and I weep.

Tuesday, October 3, 2000

PERFECTLY PERFECT

A Perfectly Perfect morning with my
Son Alejandro:
A breakfast of pancakes and eggs, with
syrup on his chin;
Walking across a crooked bridge, trying
not to fall;
Playing hide and seek at the park,
Pretending not to find him;
Watching him swing in our front yard,
shrieking with joy.

The gift of a Perfectly Perfect morning.

For Alejandro

THE SWING

It is the latest in Technology: the Seat,
made of worn hardwood,
still slightly splintered;
the braided
Rope, clinging fiercely to the oak;
the Engine, driven by muscle and slight
Exertion.

My son swings to Heaven and Laughs.

And Heaven Laughs back.

For Alejandro

Wednesday, October 4, 2000

UNDONE

Sometimes we say things we wish
Could be undone, like a ball of string a
Kitten plays with,
Or a tangled garden hose asleep in the
Garden, or a heap of fishing line
Clotted in a fist.
Yet words are different than all these,
Intangible yet more Tangible.
Heavy, they somehow float
in the Ether that
Surrounds us, unwilling to be Dismissed or
Unraveled.

THE RAIN

After many years, God decided to try again.
So one night we shared the same dream of
A rain unlike all others.

"This rain will last a long time,"
God said, "so build your boat."

We ignored God - there had been no Network
Coverage. So no boats were built.

Forty days later, God
started all over.

SEEING SOMEONE FOR THE FIRST TIME

*S*ometimes it takes years to see
Someone for the first time.
At lunch today, over a meal of warm mussels in white wine,
I saw my wife for the first time:
Her hair, short and black, laying soft behind her ears;
Her lips, rich and red;
Her eyes, desert black;
Her smile, a full moon illuminating landscapes.

The heart melts when you See.

For Leila

Thursday, October 5, 2000

OCTOBER NIGHTS

October nights were best. Seven of us would meet,
Letter jackets draped loose over worn sweatshirts.

Too young to drive, we would walk to the high school
Football game.
Past the cold cemetery,
Across fields and dark gardens,
Through burial mounds of red leaves.

And all of us, blessed by a full moon.

I didn't know it then, but
I realize it now.

Friday, October 6, 2000

THE WIND

*S*ometimes you know the Wind is trying to tell you
Something. Maybe it's a secret, to let you know
How the world works.

Or four reasons to be sad,
And eight reasons to be happy.

Or how the pyramids were
Built.

Or maybe it just wants you to learn its song,
so it will have a companion.

Saturday, October 7, 2000

PROPHET

I met a Prophet yesterday. He smokes cigars,
And washes windows for a living.

"There are only two things you need to know about God,"
he said.

"First, There is a God."

"And the second?" I asked.

"You ain't Him," he replied.

For Terry Brennan

PROPHET, REVISITED

The Prophet looked down at me from the window ledge.
"There's only one more thing you should
Know," he said.

"We are all on a river, each of us with God in our boat. God
steers, you row. You got that?"

I said I did.

"Remember, you just row. God'll take care of the rest."

He paused, and added:
"Don't forget: God Don't Row."

For Terry Brennan

Sunday, October 8, 2000

THREE HUNDRED SECONDS

*I*t's five minutes until I turn forty-two. Or Three Hundred
Seconds to listen to:
wind scattering leaves outside my
window,
my wife's slow sleep,
the air conditioner rattling the vent above our bed.

Three hundred seconds is a long time.

Monday, October 9, 2000

MEMORIES OF THE BODY

*M*aybe it was a great-great grandfather clicking his tongue
before laughing,
Or a smiling aunt, the left side of her
mouth lower than the right,
Or a forgotten uncle, shrugging his shoulders before
getting undressed,
Or a cousin, tapping with long fingers.

These are the memories of the body.

TOWER OF BABEL

We each have little tribes inside
Hidden by the organs and fed by
running blood.
Each speaks its own
Language, unintelligible to one another.

Some speak in tongues, some make
Sign language.

The Tower of Babel lives inside the heart.

THE LAKE ON MY BIRTHDAY

It is windy, still. The lake waters have turned gray
and green, and larger than the ocean. Three small boats
have disappeared; the alligator warms itself in its
Den.

And the Oaks throw moss wreaths away, like confetti,
filling the lake bottom.

Tuesday, October 10, 2000

ANGER

I left the screen door opened, and Anger came in.
His boots tracked mud on the kitchen floor, and his dirty
Hands ruined our dish towels.

I hope he leaves soon.

RECIPE

A twelve-foot wooden boat with a
discarded outboard motor,
is all it takes.

A Can of Sardines, a plastic
Jug filled with water, and a box of stale
crackers.

Four men, none of whom know the
Ocean, a rusted compass, and
a sense of
humour that finds laughter in nothing
funny.

And prayer.
Lots of prayer.

Four days later, my father had crossed
The Gulf of Mexico.

For my father, and all
Cubans, living and
Dead, who escaped
Communist Cuba

CRAZED MONKEY

The mind chatters
like a crazed monkey in a
Cage.
Or so someone once said.

Maybe if I feed mine enough
bananas it
will quiet down.

THE ANGELS

*L*ate at night, she prayed to the Virgin:
"Please protect my son, as only you can, and
forgive me my weakness."

Having said that, her raw hands released the inner
tube.

And the Angels heard her prayer, and swam to the
boy,
pushing him to safety.

For Elián

Wednesday, October 11, 2000

THE FIGHT

$\mathcal{D}$ressed in his favorite embroidered robe, undefeated Sleep
enters Francisco's room,
And tells him it's time to sleep.

Francisco says No.

Sleep steps back and regroups. Then he sings his sweetest
lullaby. It is the voice of a hummingbird.

Francisco says No, and throws down his milk bottle.

Sleep smiles and, more softly yet, sings a second verse.
The voice of a cloud, adrift.

Francisco pushes his feet straight in the air, and pulls off
Both blue socks. They join the milk bottle.

Sleep recognizes Talent. So filling
His throat with honey, Sleep sings the third Stanza:
A meadow filled with hummingbirds,
Drifting clouds, and
warm dandelions.

And Francisco, with a smile, turns onto his stomach and
Sleeps.

For Francisco

Thursday, October 12, 2000

DEVILS

One thing about Devils you can notice (if you have
Eyes):
They sit ramrod straight. Always. No Exceptions.
The other day, at the monthly board meeting, the
Devils gathered around their mahogany table.
In unison, they said: Work harder. Then you'll be Happy.

Another thing about Devils you can notice (if you have
Eyes):
Their suits are always Pressed. Always. No Exceptions.
At the last monthly board meeting, the one to my left said:
Iron your shirts. Then you'll be Happy.
They all nodded in agreement.

One more thing about Devils you can notice (if you have
Eyes):
Their shoes are always shined. Always. No Exceptions.
At the last monthly board meeting, the one to my right said:
Want More. Then you'll be Happy.
And they all grinned. White, polished grins.

One last thing about Devils:
Don't believe them.

Friday, October 13, 2000

NIGHT ICE

Walking through deep snow
my small red sled follows every
step
of our black buckled boots
that crunch
like cereal
the
crisp night ice.

OCTOBER WIND

The street was empty of all people and horses
Only cut grass filled the curbs

and white linens,
still wet, hung from
clotheslines

while a moon-filled wind
Told
scary
stories.

Saturday, October 14, 2000

CONFUSION

*C*onfusion came by yesterday morning, and
Woke me from my nap. He was wearing
a
crumpled
Seersucker suit
And selling brushes door to door.

Here again? I asked.

He brushed white lint from his shoulder.
"You're one of my best customers," he replied.

HUNGRY

 $\mathcal{T}$ he dead man woke up, stretched, and rolled his
Legs off the bed. His bedroom slippers felt warm
And snug, just as he had left them.

He smelled bacon frying in the kitchen and
Realized
he hadn't eaten in years.

Being dead can make you hungry.

LAZARUS

After 42 years
  two failed marriages
  Three children
  A functioning business
  A house in the suburbs with
          a cottage on the beach
  three honorary degrees
  the same Friday afternoon golf foursome
  and the recent presidency of his local Rotary,

Lazarus awoke, smiled, and stretching,
Slipped
his cold feet into beige slippers.

It was time for his morning coffee.

In Memoriam

to

EDUARDO FRANCO,

DREW SILVERN,

and

SCOTT CUSKADEN

Thank you for the blessing of your friendship.

Numen Press, Inc.

numen: *a divine or creative force.*

For more information on upcoming titles to be
offered by Numen Press, Inc., please contact us at:

P.O. Box 357
Winter Park, Florida 32790-0357

About the Author

Born in Matanzas, Cuba in 1958, Guillermo grew up in Cedar Falls, Iowa. He graduated from Stanford University with degrees in Economics and Political Science and has worked in the financial services industry since 1983. He lives in Winter Park, Florida, with his wife, Leila, and their two sons, Alejandro and Francisco.

Guillermo has been writing poetry since the age of eight.